SWELTERING

LABYRINTH

BY

S. OLA AJIMISAN

Cover redesigned for KDP reprint

by

Word UP

Dubai, UAE

SWELTERING LABYRINTH

S. Ola Ajimisan

First published in Nigeria in 2022

By

Royal Paraphernalia Press International Ltd

(Publishers and Publishing Consultants)

St Number's Garden, Olokola Expressway,

Ode-Etikan, Ilaje, Ondo State

Nigeria.

08136648486

ISBN: 978-978-794-053-2

DEDICATION

This collection is dedicated to the sweet and eternal memory of the griots in my life; Late Prince Number Olorunsola Ajimisan (aka the Mobile Encylopaedia), my loving father, who has continued to teach me in dreams, fantasies and revelries, for transmitting the gene of intellectual profoundness onto me through my dearest mom, Princess Esther Semilola Poroye, Oma Ologhoefoyekun, Oma ogan eluju eyi mi ma jigan-jigan naiberun omi... and to my maternal grandfather, Late Prince Johnson Arowosola Poroye who taught me how to read, write and tell every ordinary tales with extraordinary tact and finesse.

ACKNOWLEDGEMENTS

My sincere gratitude to all my teachers, members of my immediate family, my siblings, my compatriots, childhood accomplices in rebellion, all those who have shown me kindness at one passage in my life or the other and those who will still be magnanimous to me in my future rites of passage from conformity to rebellion. Thanks a bunch, for accepting and loving me with my tendentious rebellion against order that has yielded its place to disorder. Thanks again, for not despising my little efforts and my humble beginning.

CONTENTS

Dedication *iv*
Acknowledgement *v*
Content *vi*
Poet's Preface viii
JUST LIKE DEW 1
THERE SHALL BE NO PEACE 3
AWA LO KAN (THIS IS OUR CHANCE) 7
NAIJA MUST GO! 9
FIDDLERS AT THE COMMUNION 11
A FIGHT IN THE NIGHT 15
ALAINIRONU, ARA GALATIA 17
DEATH HIMSELF SHALL DIE 18
EPITAPH 20
FATE OF THE FATE BUILDERS 21
NO DAWN YET 23
THE RAIN ON THIS DERTITUS 26
OPPRESSION WILL NOT END 28
OJUMO IRE 29
AFRICA 32
WE MUST LEARN TO FLY AGAIN 34
SHEPHERDS ON SELFIE MODE 36

ODE TO THE WATER CURRENT 37
WHAT IS IN AN EMPTY ANTHEM? 38
BREWED IN NAIJA 41
POLL-TIDE SEERS AT LENTENTIDE'S EUCHARIST 43
FALSEHOOD UNCLAD 46
YEYE OSUN 48
MALOKUN (IN PRAISE OF THE DEITY OF THE SEA) 52
LOOKING BACK 53
MAN, KNOW THYSELF! 55
YES, TOGETHER, WE CAN 58
JUST PRETEND TO BE DEAD 62
EMPTINESS FOR SALE 64
GRANPA'S NATIVE NIBBLES AND PARADOXES 66
RELIGIOPRENEURSHIP 72
STILL LEARNING 74
A DANCE IN THE RAIN 78
SEMAPHORE OF THE FLOUNDERING SHIP 80
TO THE KETTLE CALLING POT BLACK 82
IF I SUSPECT YOU 85
REIGN OF THE IDIOTS AND RASCALS 86
IF THE PEOPLE STAND 88
ANOTHER HOLOCAUST LOOMING 89
JUST WITHOUT LULL 91

ON YOUR TRACK! 93
THIS TIME SHALL PASS 95
THE STAINLESS SLAUGHTER SLAB 97
VIRTUE AND VICES DON'T DIE 100
I'M OGBUULU: A POETIC HISTORIOGRAPHY 101

Poet's Preface

Moses Adejumo (Baba Sala) once entitled one of his plays Orun Mooru which means the heaven is sweltering. I have observed that when Baba Sala said that the heaven was melting under the intractable influence of the fervid sun, the situation was still bearable, as against the reality currently dawning on the citizens of the world. The world and her various man-made territorialities have been knotted together into a misleading labyrinth gnashing her teeth under the tongue of the sweltering sun of neo-modernism or postmodernism and technology. Man has stiffled and ruffled the porous peace of the world by their actions and inactions. The world is now a languishing labyrinth that is as well sweltering. When Asa, one of Nigerian controversial musicians sang "there fire on the mountain" , it was just volcanic vapour that she saw. She has not seen fire on the mountain. Now, the real fire is on the rock and the rock is Nigeria. Nigeria is melting under the heat of internal fire ignited by bad governance, purposeless leadership and man's inhumanity to man. Nigeria is now a labyrinth capable of making her citizens lose faith.

This collection betokens the poet's daily observations of the history of human progress and the attendant corollaries of the progress on humanity or the global ecosystem. The end of the world, as recorded by the Christian Holy Book, may be looming, sequel to man's insatiable tendency to tailor the world to kowtow to his tendentious whims and caprices. This also extends to all spheres of human existence such as war, security, religion, diplomacy and so on.

Characteristically, the poet does a poetic recollection and documentation of the interaction man with the world in a diction laden with copious folk tradition of his Ilaje-Etikan people. Some of the poems exemplify the poet's experimentations with novel styles evolved out of rebellion against conventions. He has made his mark by foregrounding his ideological creed that styles, anywhere in the world, are deliberate glorifications of transgressions with a view of achieving revolutonary and innovative forms that place much poetic significance and prominence on the message above conventional inhibitions called traditions. Such rebellion and transgressions against the convention are found in almost all his works, especially his latter works. They are signatures of his campaign or advocacy for the decolonisation of Contemporary African Poetry from the strangulation of Eurocentric or "Caucasoid-morphic" conventions and poetic paradigms. The experiments saw the poet writing contemporary poetry with the traditional African tale Tradition so as to achieve evolution of a poetic hybrid with global appeal to global readers. In each of the poems, the trado-cultural creed finds expression as a story waiting to be told in verses. Therefore, I have no skepticism in recommending the book for the continuation of poetic thoughts and discourses in World Literatures-in-English.

JUST LIKE DEW

When we all become news
and souls seamlessly soar away like dew
and our organs that have wrought
and bought all that we garnered and fought
for, become cast away like lifeless banana peels,
when our fleshes become marooned like eels
in the selfish sacophaguses and sail heavenward
or according to our deeds, drift conversely
hellwards,
all that will remain of our cute carcasses will be
news
of what we have done or undone knowingly or
unknowingly.
Do you seek this death and life like evergreen
pastures
in the ovary of human history or vagina of the
future?
Do you willessly wish to wane without being
remembered
like the dewdrops on the arms and languishing
limbs
of the gnomic grasses that fissle out in nimble
limps?
Man must like pastures peel away
Flesh and bones will soberly shed

their tiresome toga like shreds
and avidly retire for the threesome bed
of tempestuous torture or to good heaven be led.
Man, the doer of all deeds
sown scrupulously like seeds
on the severe soil of time
will fall off like leaves or lines,
but their deeds will bury them
like condemned carcasses of venomous vipers
who eat off the bowels of their mothers to be
livers.
So, doers die and vanish just like dew
but their deeds ages into news that outlive him
and his sinew.

THERE SHALL BE NO PEACE

There shall be no peace
This curse shall not cease
to hit and haunt
all those who make themselves pawns
in the hands of wicked leaders
and on the bosom of naked government and
power-dealers.
This rebelliously ruffled national fettle
has been indiscriminately unsettled
by those who care about themselves and not
OTHERS.
This is clueless and cruel cabals have murdered
sleep
and deserve to be swallowed deep
into the fallopian tube of joyless and peaceless
morrow
for they have plunged the poor and needy into
sorrow.

I insist that there will be no peace
to all bad leaders who have sold
this milk of humanity and fill their breasts
with milk of inhumanity to man, with love so
cold.

There shall be no peace,
I am not cursing,.
I am not hurting.
Just trying to grease
the ego of the leaders and power-craze
of those who immersed into the pool
of directionlessness and misrule.
If you curse the people
who are not thankful
to you for all your quotidian blessings
and goodwill, there is no crime.

There shall be no peace
to those who scavenge on all meat
and to all those who hoard
and steal collective wealth like horde
so that wealth will wallow in their selfish
gourds.

There shall be no peace
for those who shut down schools
and make the children of the poor roam
the schools of the streets like drifting gnomes
and like school of whales on nautical prowl.
There shall be no rest
for those who murdered with zest,

the rest of the restless oppressed.
There shall be no rest
for those who send their seeds
abroad for learning but turn to weeds
the children and wards of the pious poor
and shut eternally and remorselessly the doors
all of hope of the children of poor that their
children
may continue to make the children of the poor
barren.
Restless shall their rest eternally be.
Bitter shall their swindled sweetness turn
like the indiscriminately upturned urn.

This sweltering labyrinth that they have
constructed
with the rewards from Akeldama and damnable
debauchery
like Judas Iscariot shall spuriously sprout
curse and restlessness for their yet-to-be-born
generations
even till the dawn recompence and rapacious
reparations.
There shall be no peace and rest
for all those who pay everything
to all those who for the nation do nothing

and pay nothing to all those
who for the nation do everything.
So shall it be now and always!

AWA LO KAN (THIS IS OUR CHANCE)

For Lucky Orimisan Ayedatiwa

What is sauce for the goose
the sages say is sauce for the gander.
Many times and tides I flunk
With my sullen soul sunk
into the dungeon of daring disappointments.
I sullenly seek avid appointments
that comes and goes before it reaches me.
From the jagged root of my mind
fluctuates spasmodically some flutter
of freaky ferrocity, naggingly nudging
me to try again and again
till I dispell my diabolical disdain
from both the sacred and profane
contests with which the world has been
bethroted.
Before my resignation, I heard that tremulous
tidings:
Iwo lokan: now, at last, has come your chance.
Have you cried and shed sullen tears?
Have you been married without dowry
and without characteristic connubial bliss?
Have you failed innumerable times

without a respite and cuddle from loved ones?
Have you failed a trillion times?
Have you swum a thousand tides?
Have you tasted the sumptuous sun-burn
with his masculine scorching turns?
Have you had recrudescence of buoyant
bufetting
of the world's weighty waves without weight?
Have you continued to have multitudinous
miscarriages
that have sucked out of you, your calm carriage?
Have you therefore murdered
the tendency to try more and more?
Take a deep breath, smile to yourself as if to the
misty mirror
and muster mightily the mantra "Emi lo kan".
That is the spirit!
It is resolutely rigid
This is my chance to change
and my change to better chance.

Akure, Turning ASUU strike into blessings,

August 30, 2022.

NAIJA MUST GO!

Before I grew,
Before I knew,
When I was young,
Before I grew strong,
I used to know of
Ghana must go,
That very bag in which pride
of a nation was once betide
as a place that refused to grow.

Then, Naija was tailored
with some sense of truth
and sane thoughtfulness and lore
that guarded her land and fruits.
Ghanaians and Africans from all walks
worked in and for Naija, walking the talk
of sanity, sanctity and irresistible industry
that moved to permanent site, the ministry.

Such was the time.
Such was the tide.
Such was the tale
of a home once hale.

Now, I watch with torrential tears

flowing from my errant eyesballs,
that swells the stomach of my fears
as our workaholic women conscript
themselves to act infra-dignifying scripts
that changes the narrative from
Ghana must go to Naija must go.
How did we get here?
Mismanagement of resources and FUNDS-fare?

FIDDLERS AT THE COMMUNION

A poetic memorialisation of the ungentlemanly violence that characterised the 2022 NBA NATIONAL CONFERENCE

Standard living, standard living,
Standard living, standard nation,
If you look me up and down,
You will know that it's the truth with a frown.
Ayam a lawyer in my CUNTry
Yeah, everybody knows well,
If you look me up and down you will know it is hell.
You see, eeehn? I'm a lawyer by calling and birth
and I piously practice law with monstrous mirth.
This road to the BAR and communion altar
have been holistically hijacked by buffoons
who willingly soil the white wigs with well of oil
and our gentlemanliness determined to soil and foil.
The Kingdom of the law and *BEERring* BAR suffered *fawulens*

and the violent took it by power, by force
like loathsome documents of desirable divorce.
This road is rough
This thought is tough
Only the tough can ply it unhurt
or by stupendously swallowing the hurt.

"*Ayam* a learned gentle fellow"
You are my studious bedfellows
why can't we wittingly mellow
Our differences like budding billows
and conduct ourselves like roses on pillows?

I heard of the plundering of the communions elements
in the annual communion of the learned beings on earth.
I heard of the misconduct and perfidious dearth
that raged like the heat from *Gehena's* hearth.
It couldn't have been wrought by lawyers.
I swear, it was wrought by buffoons and "sawyers".
How could law-vaunting lads and lasses lull
themselves in such unscrupulous mull?
Anyway, thank God I didn't see the racketeering.

I only saw *Shetima's* sordid dressing
mutineering
I saw only his damnable dress code
that almost our patriotic peace corroded.
But, I also saw saws and wits in his address
If only he'll walk the talk and scorn his dress.
I have seen policemen pummelling peers
in scary scramble for bribes and meet of deers
sinisterly swindled from bloody civilians
relegated from giants to lily-livered Lilliputians
by the lame law of the land laid at the feet
of lawless lawyers and lugubriously learned
silks.
They know the law.
They speak in saws.
They have read all the books,
drank of ceaselessly welling brooks,
fetched from fresh fountains nude and raw,
but walk not the walk of the lecherous law,
lame before the rich and the rulers
but agile before the poor like measuring rulers.

You see, my people,
let's fart and forget the ripples.
Naija is incurably indiscriminate to laws
just like the iceberg that thoroughly thaws

at the sight of the sultry sun of lawlessness.
Wahala be like studying law in lawless land
like lowly NAIJA where law sentinels
now break the frangible law like eucharistic
elements.
With this, how do I courteously convince my
children
that Nigerian lawyers and lawlessness are not
kindreds?

Akungba-Akoko, turning ASUU strike into blessings, August 25, 2022.

A FIGHT IN THE NIGHT

For Demehin Oluwatosin and the Falconets,
scorned and ill-nourished by the falconers
during the 2022 Women Soccer Championship

It used to be a walk in the night
viewed through La Guma's sight
but, now a fight in the night
savoured through the senses of the Falconets
like falcons fidgeting freakishly before
bayonets.
The Falconets scorned scorching sun
to be unto their NAYshun a luminous sun.
They staked their sultry sweat to irrigate NAIJA
soccer field
but their solicitious sweat to NAIJA no heed
yield.
Only the tendentious tenacity of the eery eagle
gave them cheers and to stop them from being
feeble.
They went for a furtive fight in the night
with the opponents holding them tight
on the jugulars as they represented a coven
as hot as hellish and covetuous oven

that has starved them of attention and finance
soul and body to baptise their souls with
discountenance.
Now, their laurels lasciviously lauded
by the government that scavenges on fondling
fraud.

Akungba-Akoko, turning ASUU strike into blessings, August 25, 2022.

ALAINIRONU, ARA GALATIA

I just watched our soldiers
with their sagging shoulders
as they put the emptiness of Nigeria
on display like the thoughtless Galatians.

It just occurred to me
to write what I have seen
like John on the isle of Patmos,
the chronicle of a NAYsun's pathos.

An army torn to shreds at home,
feigning zoomed zest at the Imperial dome.
I watched with dismay
I watched in disarray
an army disunited at home
availing unity glee to the globe.

My jaws drooped as I watched
a NAYsun humbled on her knees
in-between the claws of terror-sprees
demonstrating squandered security and
ululating unity like the sea-chest's sand.
The albino's friend is sincere
to the albino, but to himself, the albino is
insincere.

DEATH HIMSELF SHALL DIE

For Mrs Eunice Kudehinbu, aya Aheri Oliro, Aya'ba Oluhapen meji eyi e e gbedon je agwa-gwa.

I had a dreary dream
I crossed the sweltering stream
I fondled the breasts of the wonderment
yet to ripe like the withering wilderness.

Death laid lifelessly lame
with all his humongous hate and fame
of being the end of all things
and of being the eater of all dreams and beings.

He is the end of all beings and indeed,
the end of himself and his hurtful deeds
Lie himself shall lifelessly lie
Death himself shall searingly die.

Death shall be muffled in disgrace
together with his twin brother, the grave,
cast into the cervix of the fiery furnace
and those who do good shall be saved.

Though, we wastefully wail here
death will wither and wail in the hereafter.
So, those who lose their dotting darlings today
should themselves console that death is profane.

They should take solace in the firm faith that

death himself shall die and be cast into
inextinguishable
hearth-dungeon in condemnation impregnable
and ineffable
that good people will eternally live and chant
the praise of *Edumare*.

EPITAPH

To the great beyond, as you go
and your soul like vapour seamlessly blown,
we earnestly entreat you to sleep softly,
tread tenderly the jasper-coated thoroughfare.

Again, as you bid this world that is bizzare
adieu towards the lamb-illuminated hectares,
sweet is your never-resting rest
relished restively with zany zest.

Here rest the relentless remains
of dotting darling who strived to maintain
her strong grip on the jagged jugulars of
rectitude
and has now been translated onto transcendental
altitude.

Akure, turning ASUU strike into blessings,
August 26, 2022.

FATE OF THE FATE BUILDERS

Prof. Emmanuel Osodeke

Sadly, poliTICKSians have grown fat
like the gluttonously fed fads,
even by building but themselves
like the dearth-betide books on idle shelves.

They fatten fastidiously at the expense of real
builders
who leave their seeds to build an emancipated
state
that starves her intellectuals rabbis and feeds
her palace plunderers and pen racketeers.
This ASUU strike is the certificate of leaders
who wittingly and unwittingly starve readers
who stay sailing the ocean of thoughts
that the nation may marry not knowledge-drought.

The farting fools who rule the wise grow chubby
like the alluvium-enriched robust rubbies
while the conscience of the nation grow gaunt.
Before the starving scribes, the farting fools flaunt
minty meat, gulp gins and wines of debauchery,
that feed fat furlough treasury of political
chicanery,

hatched and incubated in the incubator of
tomfoolery.

I weep out my receding eye balls
as our poliTICKSians gulp like galls
the national cake only on paper pages
but oligarchic on the table reeking of brigandage.
What is national about the cake that is not
democratised
but is rather exclusively extorted by ticks who
pauperise
the soil that breeds the seeds
and cakes cornered by the crooks?
Even Lucifer and Mephistopheles
may more mercy or oblations obtain
in the armament of the fervid furnace than these
villains
for they have defecated into the life fountains
from which they once drew the water of life.

Akure, Turning ASUU strike into blessings,
August 27, 2022.

NO DAWN YET

Indeed, no dawn yet for Naija,
a nation that cannot raise funds
or get loans to fund university education
but can raise funds for frivolous forms framed
for
the anointing of the next brood of mutineers
that will continue as plunderers and racketeers
of the Commonwealth that is uncommon for
the next four years of groping in gratuitous
dusk.

Numerically, Naija boasts of hundreds of
tongues
and tribes that differ in creeds lores and
prolonged
chauvinism, yoked together by lecherous lords
only for the ploy to increase ease and eggs,
there are discernibly "two peoples"in her
warped womb:
we, the economically hapless have-nots hauling
hellish hullabaloos at one another all because
of bullying boors who care alone about
themselves

and they that divide us along ethno-religious
borderlines
to increase their eggs and fatten their "Jerugbe"
bags.

Tears flood my eyes like the tide that sweeps
off a mansion
and a sea of malignant mutiny meanders
through the thoroughfare
of soul-less solicitude in me and I feel like
tearfully taking
cruel kalashnikovs and assail the fucking folks
for their
indifference to the plight of Naija, the mother
writhing in throes
by her hellish heirlings hunting high and low
to breed and multiply multitudinous woes
for the mirthless multitude, married to merciless
misery.

Education, the inner eyes of every sane clime
is comatose in Naija, no one is convening
thought-provoking confabulations that will ease
her off the die-hard dusk that has held her
hapless

like a plague, foisted on her by rudderless
rulers,
but the political musketeers meet dusk and dawn
in bargaining for the selection of the chief
musketeer.
If these thieving tetrarchs and their broods of
vipers
are not swept off by the volcano of Masses'
wrath,
like hurtful hurricane, there'll be no dawn,
but dusk always, till rapture and *Amaggedon*.

I see the birth of a dawn ripening with wrath
from the
impoverished masses mercilessly mangled by
the profiteers
who cumbersomely carouse themselves like the
volunteers
on reckless rescue, riddled with worthless
racketeering.

THE RAIN ON THIS DERTITUS

In memoriam of Mama Grace Akeredolu,
mother of many children from different
borderlines

I know that there shall be restful rain
and soothing splendour shall shine again
on this drab detritus after the sultry sun
of placid platitude that lingers like the gun
and the showers refreshing rising to the moon
like the bride rejoicing at the birth of connubial
bloom.

Though, confounded and contused we must be,
certainly our dazed detritus may later see
the birth and burgeoning of the beatific sea
of relief and hefty hope into which
the sole of our souls will be bewitched.

Our souls will be beatifically baptised
with wooly water of right recompence
commensurate with our teaching toils
like the seeds that germinate and sprout on
supple soil.

The hot-seat that is today chronic and cosy
shall sooner or later give way for the one that's rosy..

Then, will the boat of our arcadian arch-enemies,
political plunderers wobble and ceaselessly capsize.
Then, will Esu Elegbara torment them beyond size.
Rejoice unhinged, oh kindreds,
for there shall soothingly shower
on us relishing rain of reeking reward with power.

Akure, turning ASUU strike into blessings,
August 28, 2022.

OPPRESSION WILL NOT END

As long as you live
As long as you laugh
with your oppressors
and with your tormentors,
your livened laughter with
your ominous and hell-bent oppressors
will make you traitorous transgressors
and embolden your oppressors
to continue the opiating oppression.

If you must be free,
from oppression spree,
you must be ready to disagree.
You must be ready to be a rebel
against the domineering infidels
that strip you of your dignity
like prostitutes at the brothels
ridden by men and beasts
of sizes till tarrying infinity.
End therefore, your oppressors
before they endlessly end you
like a docile deer or lame ewe
led to the abattoir remorselessly.
Freedom is snatched, not negotiated.

OJUMO IRE

For Mama Janet Orimisan Okun-omo the Amazon that conquered the sea by hard work.

Intended as a performance poem to the accompaniment of "Asa's Ojumo ti mo" or any song of preference of the performer.

The dawn is born
An infant dawn is birthed
as the dusk is berthed
on the anchor and dockyard of yesteryears.

The soaring and dutiful dove
born as twin, close to the fingers like glove
come, roost on my head and shoulders
like mystically muffled gracefully gyrating
grasses gyrating to the mystical music
of the innocent breeze of the new dawn.

The dawn has returned the pilgrimage
of piety in the elusive realm of yester-days
and I have found fortune and pearls in-between
the limbs of the young and never-dying dawn.

I earnestly entreat you, kindreds
to earnestly entreat your children
to look through their windows
an be immersed like willing widows
into the serene splendor
of the luminous dawn with candour.

Wake freely from sullen slumber,
take thoughtfully dauntless dominion
open your eyes to dare the gas of the onion
dare the riotous royal minions
as you rejoice at birth of a pregnant dawn.
Walk willingly through the laurel-doned lawn
not like worthless worms and pawny prawns.

Explore the dew-doned and mild meadows,
comb through the pot-bellied dawn
to mid-wife the day's dearly treasure
deckecked for you without worthless measure.
Did you wake from the wrong wrung of your
bed?
Brighten up your face,
daringly dispell doleful daze
as you soundly sail through the hefty haze.

Is your head bowed and drowned

into the fallopian tube and cobwebs
of doubt and irate incertitude?
Wake up!
Brace up!
Move on!
Adorn yourself with the taunting toga
of hope like dottingly decorated yoga
dancers and sing insidiously to yourself
that you can, and will wade through like an elf,
the iceberg of impossibility ahead of you.

Though you went to sleep
helpless like the ship on the abysmal deep,
though you lay languishing like the crusty
cucumber
on the languorously languid sea floor,
encumbered
on all sides and tossed tumultuously by the
jugulars of the ocean,
You will live lissomely like lilies to tell your
tales like the crustaceans.

AFRICA

Africa, our Africa,
Africa of whom my mom sings
Africa, the land that glad tidings brings.
Africa, our Africa,
the land and folks vaster than Antarctica
Africa of die-hard cultures
that kowtows to no vultures.
We are dark-skinned
Yet, not dark-brained
or of weak body and souls
like the blood-thirsty bullies and ghouls.
Give us the field of Europe
and we will master it like antelopes.
Grant us the American ivory towers
and we will excell with will-powers.
Avail us of the Asian tracks
and we'll with laurels return without cracks.
Ours is the colour that bred others.
Ours is the strength that upholds others.
Ours is the blood that cross-fertilises the ova of others.
Ours are the shoulders shouldering the world
like the tripod and the soldiers' swords.
Ours are the hairy fields decked with strands

behind which the pubes of the world is veiled
and stands
Though, the scars of the heydays of slavery
our breasts and souls monogrammed
yet for great loft we are wired and programmed.
I am sure that if the plundering

I mean if soul floundering,
If the negro-decked ship foundering
that attended the land of the sepia
had attended those of the carnivorous
Caucasians,
Nothing but charred carcasses
or floundering foetus will there remain.
Nothing but intellectual frailties will there
remain.
Despite the whips and the porous prejudice,
Africa will rise like the Phoenix
and metamorphose into paradise.
Arise, Africa, unite and roost
even without external boost,
take your place with ancestral grace
among nations and tongues on the global space
as done before by your able ancestors.

WE MUST LEARN TO FLY AGAIN

For Odia Ofeimun

We were once soaring eagles.
We were never incapacitated and feeble.
We shed each day our pious plume
and retool our kits and perfume
that the world again may return our costume.

Before, other neighbours were
at our table, solicitious supplicants.
Now, to the inconsequential, we are applicants
for the clogs on the eagle's nest
has her strenuous strength suppressed.
She now has her head buried in the mud
like the fraill-framed and ailing mudskipper.
She now limps down the lonely path without a
skipper.
The soaring eagle has yielded her health to
starvation.
The whole world pities her but she pities not
herself.
The world rejects even as she rejects herself and
her own.

Her wings were clipped without brace
and now at her neighbours' mercy and grace.
What is the antidote
For corroding this episode?
What is the way out
of this threatening tide and bout?
She must learn to fly.
She must learn to ply
again her characteristic noble flight.

SHEPHERDS ON SELFIE MODE

Shut down all the schools
Close down all the pools
Sell out all the collective tools
and begin to pose like a fool
in order to fill the my empty
brain, foreign accounts and pockets
that my treasure may magnificently skyrocket.

We own the ocean and the spacious sea.
We own the mountains of arable Arabia.
We have muffled Swiss and British banks
with weighty worth of kneeling Naira
who has surrendered her pride to China
that others may have a lot
to eat without satisfaction.
We do not care whether or
not your face shows in the camera
We care about nobody even as we care
about nothing but ours like lecherous hare
simply because we are on self-seeking selfie
mode.
That and nothing but that is our covetuous code.

ODE ON THE WATER CURRENT

For Mama Esther Okun-omo, Oma Gbabijo Olorere, Ikoloma lobi-leri.

Today, a song I croon
Today, I bear a tune
In praise of the water current,
the kindred spirit of the torrent
that causes caressing swoon
as he sweeps across the pool.
With hands invisible, he calls the sand
to dance to his music and command.

Man with his hefty hands to him succumbs
Like lifeless leaves at the mercy of the storm
and like lordless louts with feeble forms.
Who will not fear thee?
Who dare you to a spree?
You have no hands and do not move
But the skillful swimmers into perditions you shrove.

WHAT IS IN AN EMPTY ANTHEM?

For TOBI AMUSAN, OUR HEROINE, PATRIOT AND ATHLETE, AND ALL THOSE WHO, AGAINST ALL ODDS, STILL REPRESENT THE NATIONS THAT DO NOT REPRESENT AND VALUE THEM

What, I ask, is our empty anthem?
What again, I ask, is in our phony item,
the pledge, the flag and the cosmetic coat of arms
when we pledge to serve a nation that cares
not about our existence and phony fitness?

Yesternight, a female athlete swore
to blaze abroad our national lore.
But the idle instructors who feed
on the athlete's glory pay no heed.
She talked of her skillful strength
but the ministry's folks talk of their pockets' length.

Determined against all crosses and odds,
the athlete bore her haughty cross and rod

and set to tell the track-bound tales
with no kindreds to hear and hail.
At last, a harvest of garlands and laurels
now arrogated to the carefree "MEANistry"
of Sports and Youths UNDERdevelopment
interested not in the athlete's angry angst
but in her tale of lonely and shepherdless valour.
At the race's dreary death,
at the lone and forsaken dread
of being alone before the universal audience

she was deserted to the cacophonous ambience
greeting her heeding hearing from people who
were not hers.

Only her suppressed sobs and traceless tears
toggled
a sound that impregnated the silence of
conspiracy
from the nation that craved the athlete's
patriotism
but with nothing, not even cheers to offer in
return.
With rebellious insistence, I ask again and
again,
What is in the animating anthem of a "CUNTry"

that is stingy to a patriot in need of her beer
and also held back from HER, her chilly cheers?
Come not for my head, for I'm not of your
region.
Go instead for the heads of your loathsome
legion.
A nation that cares not about the feelings of
citizens
Does not deserve the loyalty and allegiance of
the netizens.

BREWED IN NAIJA

I am the new wine
brewed not for the swines
I am the home-brewed Burukutu gin
refined for the palaces and kings.

I am the indispensable cornerstone
hewn from gems, not limestone.
I am the imprenable knowledge-store
once relegated, but now at the core.

I am the voice once berated
now the choice the world awaits.
I sing, not like the caged bird
I croon, not like the cowed cricket that chirps.

I gladden my nervous neighbours
with home-made rhythms of fervour.
I gird myself with hearty hope
scorning the intoxication of the dope,
affirming always that the world will not sit
like the iceberg of the still silt
until she is lost in the rhythm of my mellifluous
musings.

If she sat before my mesmeric musings,
her sitting soul will be immersed in my tireless tidings.
The world, I insist, will not rest
The universe starved of zest
until my song is relished and heard

like the soothing ointment on Aaron's beard.

I am tough and hard
I am a home-made bard
Bred in Naija
Bred for Naija
Toughened by Naija
for the soaring street credibility
that unearths pompous possibility.

Akungba-Akoko, turning ASUU strike to blessings, August 5, 2022.

POLL-TIDE SEERS AT LENTENTIDE'S EUCHARIST

For Segun Omosule

Elections are here again
a tide to tirelessly bargain
for the tide for the sacred and profane.
At poll-tides, everyone is a seer
In all frankness, every kindred is queer.
So I am
I too eat yam
spiced with corn and cassava
from Baba Adan, like the casanover.

I am a prophet
I too crave profit
from my prophepreneurship
like the entrepreneurship
carefree about whose mother is maimed
Or whose heritage is illegitimately claimed.
Man must surely survive
Wary women must be revived
If not by boring book
probably by curtly crook.

Be careful this season,
my kinsmen, for just a reason:
Lions and lionesses prowl,
haunt, hunt and greedily growl
unchecked on this street
dishing out fake PROFIT-sees

Like communion creed and seeds.
Do not, dear brethren, navigate this street,
Better still, choose your belief
wisely with heinous hesitation and disbelief.
You may be lucky to buy vain verity
that is barren to human clarity.

You may be unlucky to pay for truth
and still sail homeward with untruth.
One who never bought "na lie",
in this sweeping season of see-and-buy
will never buy "na true".
Take and swallow that without hue.
I have a charm with which to puncture lies.
Just two thousand and twenty-three incisions
carefreely cut across your pubes without
precision

It must be at night
like a black market
bought without trust and insight.

I too prophesy
Even blind bats and prophepreneurs prophesy
of things and tidings to be or not to be
like the sentinels gambling with Jesus'
"jalabiyya".
The blood of a prophets runs in my veins.
If I don't hear from the Jewish God,
I will consult oracles.
I must hear and prophesy
by fire, by force.

Come not to thank me
if my PROFIT-sees come true.
Come neither for me
if my PROFIT-sees bear futility.
It is just marginal propensity and utility
Thank Providence, I have no church
Just my stomach giving me lurch.

Akungba-Akoko, turning ASUU strike to blessings, August 5, 2022.

FALSEHOOD UNCLAD

Better is it for the truth
to intractably troll nude
than for falsehood to ride rudely
especially where and when falsehood
freely frequent, in lace-ladden toga,
the thoroughfare of nationhood.

Falsehood's twenty-year race
is truth's merry-go-round pace
Humanity will not romance peace
Where falsehood and her mouthpiece
carelessly carouse in affable affluence
like blooming bubbles in the confluence.

Tell those who clad themselves
with the togas of others' ordeals,
like the cocooned chameleons
That shame will at last,
be their loathsome lots
as they fruitlessly fester and rot.

Tell those who wrap themselves in mangrove
forest and there-from fire arrows
at unsuspecting unlookers that

descendants of darkness will roam
the streets unclad like frail foam
when darkness, their ailing ancestor dies
clad with nothing to clad but lies.

Tell the wormy world
the bad deeds we do
and the good deeds we undo
either clad us with worthy tattoo
like voodooists vying voraciously
for ripening reward or unclad us
like cancerous cysts corroded by acidic antidote.
Do not come and ask me
where lies go when they die
or the whereabouts of the soul
of truth in the hereafter.

Ode-Etikan, turning ASUU strike to blessings,
August 6, 2022.

YEYE OSUN

I tarry at your abode
even as I languish and grope
I languorous lay like forage
and the harem in Alaafin's palace
I sprawl before you in awe
and before you, I lay with my flaw.
I have flaw with my lore and yaw
but your state is regal and without slur.

I stand mesmerized and bewildered
Like leaves, flora and fauna, withered
and yet expectant of your bounties
devoid of festering fetters and boundaries.
I earnestly entreat you to open your womb
and engulf me like a flake trapped by a bomb.
Open up, I beseech you, your bounteous bank

To do obeisance to you, I relegate my rank
I pray thee, through me, flow
that I may, like riverside orchard, grow.
To me "revelatorily" reveal your beauteous
barrels
as I genuflect with all my garlands and laurels
that I may be bedecked by your pearly beauty

and for its sake, renounce my dauntless duty.
Fill me with lavishly leading and learned lines
Cause me to be in lissome line and let lines
Fall freely for me in pleasantly pristine places.

Open up the vast vestige of your wealthy womb
let me it be immersed like in it like in the tomb
and deck me, I pray, with your gorgeous gems
as the clement soil nourishes the sinking stems.
Hear and grant my subtle supplications
Like human employers, stamp my application.
In you finds the world no emptiness
Same way you harbour no numb selfishness.
I eulogise you that my Oliver-Twist listless
litany
may be approved like that of sisters of Bethany,
not as a grudgingly given Greek gift
but because you desire not my rancorous rift.

You are *Osun sende-se*, the owner and custodian
of the alluvial treasure base and booty-yard,
the owner of the towering, pearly and coral
comb,
with which the world combs her haughty hairy
head.

Yours is the fond fountain of the antidotal
herbal concoction
in which the world willfully wallows without
woeful conditions.
Stamp you, o mother of all good gifts, all my
wordless wrangle
that my path and soul be not betide by woes and
entangled.
Yours is the womb that birthed the wide world
yours is the creative and procreation-induced
word
that forms the word that form forming lores.
Your is the womb that begets global swoon
Your coral and alluvial beads are tokens of the
silver spoon
with which the world feed and fill themselves.
Yours is the ineffable nostril that exhales breath
of life
that grows trees and creeping creatures.
You are the world's everything.
Only the doolally who know you not,
do call you mere shallow water, neither cold
nor hot.

Yours is the coral comb with which the world
combs her head

Yours is the flower stigma that fertilises the
world's pollen
and your, sincerely is the world's adornments'
and food store.

Ode-Etikan, turning ASUU strike to blessings
August 7, 2022.

MALOKUN (IN PRAISE OF THE DEITY OF THE SEA)

I stand on the slippery sand
helplessly hauled to your chest
by *Edumare's* endless command
like little birds on nasty nest
lost in the reverie of the wonders of your store.
Malokun Ogbolu Oteteweere
the littoral lord of mighty mystiques
as my humble heart harbours no antic,
you are the one that is as vast as vastness itself.
You feed men without raucous ranting
and have offered your chubby chest
for men as for birds on the needful nest.
Malokun, you are worthy of my veneration.
Oteteweere, you are worthy of my genuflection
When you fended for me,
I was chubby and robust.
When you stopped providing,
I irredeemably grew gaunt
sequel to my impetuousness.
Malokun, fetch fortune for me
that I may quickly quip treasure.
Deity of the sea,
I earnestly entreat thee
to tailor treasure to the threshold
of my house, that I may amass gold.

LOOKING BACK

I lasciviously like looking back
even with all my moody lack
not because I still live in the past
after all, I have run fastidiously fast
and toughened by the loony and lonely race
placed and orchestrated for me by faithful fate.
I have run riotously with gregarious grace
that my legendary laurels may swallow
disgrace.

As I go, I ponder halt
On how to become a sane stalwart
Against all odds, I avoid
looking back for fearsome fear
of becoming a pillar of salt
or being dastardly devoured by bullying bears
lurking lividly beneath bountiful warts.

Rebelliously, looking back I dare
as I age, learn, unlearn, relearn and fare
through the haughty hurdles and and loathsome
longueurs
with their tardy and untoward toil, rigour and
languor.

For clinging clandestinely to the hurt and hate of
the past
One looking back is an outlandish outcast.
But, for gatitude's sake, looking back is fun
that outlasts the universe and world's sinking
sun.
I will not look back at my past, brood like a
viper
or contemplate suicide by sniper
that I will not become a pillar of salt.
Looking back, always your gifts in me will I
exalt.

Ode-Etikan, turning ASUU strike into blessings, August 8, 2022.

MAN, KNOW THYSELF!

For Ola-Oluwa Omosele

"Man, know and define thyself",
So says the creed of epistemology.
I dare ask, who are you, beyond Biology?
Today, I charge you to differently define
yourself, not as the world your life confines.
I am the amphibious and salt
Of the world that thaws without a halt.

I am the male eagle with the Brobdingnangian wings
that causes tsunami in the vast sky with its rings.
I am the dearly dolphin dottingly decked tidings
that sweetens and smoothens the cooked world
not with rupturing rods but with witty words.
I am the towering, fruit-doned and iridescent iroko
of the desert whose adventurous roots go loco,
through trillion mines
through trillion miles
to be bountifully beatified, self-irrigated,
Illuminating and irrigating others
fragrant fruits for food to those who dare to crave,

too tough and intractable for the gory grave.
I am the sheltering Araba
on whose shoulders flying creatures crave shield
and shelter.
In my bosom, they have found a buckler
and in-between the talons of roots

have creeping creatures found food.
I am the lone and unquenchable light
on an invincible and invisible candelabrum
that illuminate the paths of others like the
charted album.
I was built and branded rugged
because fate embedded in me a nugget.

I have not come to bully you
Like the bear bullying the ebullient ewe
I have not come to flaunt
I have not come to taunt
Like the Big Brother in Naija
I have only called for a feast of self-appraisal
I have only orchestrated a festival of thoughts
that those who stand may take heed
lest they grumble
lest they crumble
lest they fumble

lest they rumble
irredeemably under the ruffling rubbles.
Even, a drunkard submerged in beer-bottles
beats his chest and mumbles "I am the son of Lagbaja".
Verily, the world defines each figure
but the figure must figure out his figure with vigour.
Don't come for me and mine
because of the poser from my mountainous mines.
Just come out and before the world's camera yourself define.

YES, TOGETHER, WE CAN

Orunmila sat under hat of the Oda tree
at Ile-Ero in Ugbomekun
as majestic Okun liri and Malokun
and the children thronged him on all sides
as for a space they each throttled
as for a stump they all struggle
to give ears to his sagely tales
He sure, had a lot for sale
"Sage, tell us a tale",
rang rancorously their chorusing chants
swallowing alive the village's silent rants.
Ela cleared his hoarse voice
and decided that night for a wordless tale.
His croaky-but-firm voice raped and
impregnated
the silence of that noisome night.
His sigh tore the toga of the furnace-lit
dark paths in the hearts
of the children and Ugbomekun.
"Children of Oramfe, the landlord
of the house built of nothing but fire,
Children of Ohongangan Obamaken,
Kutukutu, king of Ugbo
tonight, there'll no tailoring tales,

as I characteristically do, but I'm hale.
But I have a few riddles to ask you all.
Whether or not you can
unriddle my ripe riddles
Just chorus tenaciously,
yes, we can, together.
That's for tonight!"
His silent voice rang.
Now I start!
Do you know that:

If we are absolute
If we are resolute
We can can a can without gloves
Mountains we'll move
Rocks we'll shrove
Seas we'll conquer
Challenges we'll swallow
In fear and lack we'll never wallow?
Yes, we can together!
rang the choral response of the children.

Do you know that
When we are tired,
Even though we are fired,
Our sleep will be sweet

As confidence will our sorrow sweep
and our joy and strength born again
and greater things than before we can do?
Yes, we can, together!

Do you know that this tough
Odan tree that shelters us
from both sun and moon
Can yield to our collective
push and be marooned
in the stomach of the
sea even in a wink?
Do you know that you instruct
the mesmeric mountain of Ora
Just with concerted self-willed
decree even without aura?
Yes, we can together!
Rang again the masterfully mustered musings.
Do you know that we can put
these daring descendants
of Agesinkolu on the run
by backing our collective confession with
actions?

Do you know that we can tend and rule the
world

through the pious power of our word?
Do you know that patience and persistence,
we can can the world and furl it into our
pockets?
Do you know that by wondrous will power,
we can push Jericho walls and Babel's tower?
Do you know that we can roast Kilimanjaro and
like yam tubers and invite the world to feast on
it with us?
Yes, we can, together!
The children chorused again.
Whatever is conceivable
is not far from doable.

"No more tales tonight.
Go, each of you,
conquer and tame the lion in your zoo
By declaring that you can!"
Rang the swansong of his word with a caveat
too wan.

Ode-Ugbo, turning ASUU strike into blessings,
August, 13, 2022.

JUST PRETEND TO BE DEAD

When you are choked and dreaded,
by life, its certitude and incertitude
Close your yearning eyes
and pretend to be dead,
see who will offer your kids bread
and heartily mourn you sincerely.

If you are man or woman enough
Tarry enough on the bulky bier
Let them can you like corned beef
and be let into the grave's steep
and see how many kindred will tarry at the wake
in your honour or shed tears that are fake
watch wittingly and carefully those whose
epitaphs are phony
or reliable and trustworthy like a penurious
pony.
You will be shocked as those who vow
to stand by you and yours will be the first
to unfurl their insatiable and irate thirst
towards your hard-earned heritage and wife
as though you never mattered to them in life.
I swear, Africans love their loved ones

more in death than in life.

All the pillow-weight pledges and vows
made like imams sanctifying their cows
before disuniting their heads from the body
made by the survivors die and journey with you
in the grave.
Your kids may even be treated and tended like
indentured slaves

by those who rode on your benevolent bosoms
and shoulders.
They may be pelted by the inloco parentis with
bullying boulders.
Such is life, when all the helpers fail and
comfort flee
or activate the mode of a glee and stingy spree.

Mahintedo, turning ASUU strike into blessings, August, 13, 2022.

EMPTINESS FOR SALE

Do not, my brother, I entreat you, advertise your emptiness
Do not, my sister, I beseech you, showcase your ignorance
Do not tell the world that you are a noisome nuisance
a replica of Faustus Karamo, who sat before global gaze
to spew silly , dishonourable and bombastic banters
from both sides of his nuzzle-like
honourable mouth like an ill-bred ranter.
Do not stand in the market place
to indiscriminately exemplify a disgrace to your race.
"Oghun erun ei den apa".
A foolish and uncultured fad
Should know when and how to talk like a honourable lad.
If you have to have no words
potent enough keep mute
instead of mounting the hallowed
pulpit to openly defecate worms

and bruise again already healing or festering
sore or be rude.
The beauty of oration is knowing when and
when not to talk.
Silence is no longer golden
especially when it molten.
Brevity is the oxygen on which oration survives.
Verbosity is corrodes the soul of wit.
Those who are paid to insult the kings
or justify the ruthless rape of the future of their
kins
should know that power is as fragile as an egg
The word too, is as frangible as an egg under the
legs.
Once it is knackered and shattered,
it refuses to be garnered and gathered.

Mahintedo, Turning ASUU strike into blessings, August 15, 2022.

GRANPA'S NATIVE NIBBLES AND PARADOXES

Intended as a Performance Poem

For Pa Alfred Ajimisan Ojaabogun

Grandpa, my mzee and pantheon-saint sat
under the apagha tree.
As Ị did obeisance on my knees,
He opened the door of his mouth
to let the world laugh at his
withered teeth like louts
and sang a song with vigour and clout.
As he mumbled the song
he struggled with the kola
in his mouth with his ridges and tongue.
The song rang:
Apagha t'oma ino re kono
Orisa ma gba mi oma te ooo...
I soon masterfully learnt the
tremulous tune and tune tunefully along.
After the song, he cleared his throttled throat
and began to reel out his native nibbles.
Although I divorced my book and pen
during the thought-provoking transfiguration
but the little I mustered changed my calibration.

His words ululated undulatingly
caged and deflowered the
virgin peace of the night.
His vaultless voice illuminated without light.
Now, lend me your erring ears, grandson!
He said in frantic and strident tune thus:
He who buys my thought
buys a calabash of honey
full of and bedecked with money
and for that purpose, made tough.
S/he has bought a coat of all colours
made for all seasons and climes
full of adorable adornments and lines.

Away from soft talks to hard talks
that fatten the tree-trunks and stalks.
Too much word fills no basket.
Brattish brevity is the casket
of verbosity and verbosity
is the casket of brevity.
Those who crave longevity
do not scorn the ailing and aged
or else they will be like birds caged.
When you open your mouth,
do not speak like that LAI-ing lout in the ROCK
for it is capable of cowing your luck and lock.

Do not talk like that loquacious lout,
The Senior Advocate of Nonentities, SAN, the tout.
Do curse and do not pray
but ensure that your mouth
does not indulge in idleness
because, what constitutes curse at an end
constitutes prayers at another end.

Those who crave sound health
do not scorn victims of ill-health
for we are all victims of either
ill-health or lack of wealth.
We all are casualties
either dead or "Godotly" awaiting funerals
including the sedulous sentries and God's generals.
Those who covetuously crave happiness
must not be harbingers of other's unhappiness.
Those who want to live long
must not attempt to bear all burdens
or please women in all things.
Even God that created them does not
seem to please in their church minds.
He gave them origin body parts

they still lust after artificial artifacts.
He gave them pure and unadulterated beauty
yet they crave cosmetics and plastic duty.
Do not die before your death all because
you want to gift an insatiable
woman harvest of orgasms.
Do not seek to win arguments with fools
lest you become a farmer without tools.
If you lost a battle,
do not be rattled.
Do not brood
rather, try to retool
You will win in subsequent jostle.
Those who are desperate to win all
end up in most cases, embrace fall.
If you must marry,
If you must tarry
marry not a nagging woman
lest you become a murderer or a victim.
If your neighbour is boasting
about his capability to ignite war
tell him this truth that is nude and raw:
Wars, like the furnace do not spare
those who carelessly kindle them.
Tell him too that wars, peace, joy and happiness
are as empty and delicate as emptiness.

Do not inherit your ancestors burdens
and their hanging hostilities against others,
for you have your own life to live and lose
and query for your deeds to answer at the close
of the dawn of reckoning and dust of torment
for everything good deed or the trouble you
forment.
To break Grandpa's monotonous monologue
and transpose the tenor discourse to a dialogue,
I interjected, "thanks for everything, gracious
Grandpa".
"Do not thank me or thank others for everything
for thanks for everything is the tactful
and subtle way of thanking him for nothing",
Retorted grandpa as a way of dispelling
distraction.
Tell those sell sand to swindle kinsmen
of their hard-earned money that they too
will be paid with stones and led to their
Waterloo.
The world is a crafty chameleon
with innumerable attires in her invisible
wardrobe
and changes with time and tide a trillion
times in a nanosecond and those who hope
to farm the world must craftily cope

with her dynamism and vainglorious
vicissitudes.
The world begot, as Siamese twin, certitude and
incertitude.
There is no empowerment without avid
armament
and there is no impoverishment without
disarmament.
To conquer your enemies,
you need energy and synergies
You have to disarm your foes
in other to surmount your throes.
If you ever seek to grow,
learn to characteristically step on toes.
Then, will you grow and glow.

RELIGIOPRENEURSHIP

I built my hut on the awkward head of the
streets
that with my eyes and mind greeted
with the all "preneurships" evolved
by men in order to have his needs enveloped.

Having learnt of pussypreneurship,
prophepreneurship, festipreneurship,
poepreneurship, miraclepreneurship,
gossipreneurship, beggarypreneurship,
banditopreneurship and stripreneurship.
I thought I had learnt enough
until I learn again in ways too tough
for my moody and tough thoughts.

I see, daily as mortal men
take raving religion into the wealth-smith den
of foxes and preying predators
thus metamorphosing into capitalistic gladiators.

Men metamorphose mightily from piety
to probable profiteering.
Men of gods grow greedily gregarious
with hunger-induced racketeering

and religious profligacy too contumacious
to shepherd onto sanity by the author of all
creeds.
It dawned on me mendaciously that most men

are called not by the author but by their greed.

STILL LEARNING

Be not surprised
Be not surpassed
by ill-nourished negligence
or deaden your intelligence
by pristine pride and porous pomposity
for like is bigger than the biggest university
The best of teachers is still learning
the strongest of giants is, too, leaning
on others for a benevolent brace
nurtured by piloting Providence and grace.

If you do not learn
you will wallow in ignorance and lies.
If you do not earn,
you will wobble and die.
I am a libral learner too,
in fate and nature's classroom.
I am still learning the rope
As I learn, I grope
through the thoroughfare of hurdles
full of paradoxes and ripe riddles.
In fate's class, we are phony pawns and fiddles.

Daily, I am earning
Daily I am learning
with trottering and tracing steps
through life's flight of steps
lhigh and sloppy as skyscraping staircase
I copy and compete with no one in the race.
I trotter through the terrace
with emptiness as my brace
as I fumble through scalding streets
with weighty wardrobe without sweets.

I lean on sweltering swing
too thirsty for my spring
as I fallow through fallowing fount
always with staggering steps.
I languish lividly through paltry path
that snakes into the crooked path of vanity,
falling and rising as I fare,
hopping and hoping as I dare,
till the thwarting sun of righteousness arise
and till the teachers tailor my path aright.

Till we die
Till we lie
and gallivant gracefully astray
fester and fissle like vapour, away,

we'll not stop learning.
We'll keep earning
as we gallop gracefully
and fare furtively, penitently and faithfully
to the gulping graveward cave
like antelopes galloping towards the cocooned
cage
without finesse but with wayward rage.

Every teacher is a learner
and every learner is teacher.
Every earner is a learner
and learner is an earner
all fervently finagling learning,
all fathoming out earnings
furtively from fathomless fount
as towering as a mawkish mount
of life, time and space.
Life is a riotoud race
and you cannot run on your neighbours' lane
or race at his panting pace.
We are all sprinters.
We are all spinsters
all flying frolicsomely like splinters
like the lone, lame duck, taking her bath

and like ailing antelopes aping towards the
trapward path
as we waywardly wriggle with weight.
You will only stop learning
You will only stop earning
Till we, learning and earning
all snake slowly on graveward race
towards the gracious grave.

A DANCE IN THE RAIN

For Chief Benjamin Olomidegun CEO of High Tide Marine, PortHarcourt and the Oluweri Magboojo of Etikan Land.

My neighbour tilled the world dauntless
bejewelled like a dotting duchess
She wore the world wingless under her finery
and in-between her laps like the brooding hen
and never wanted the world to tilt asunder from her pen
I told the neighbour who wore
the thirsty terrains of the world
like her wrapping skirt like an eyesore,
dancing daintily on freaky fringe of a gory gore
to bear in mind life's lovable constraints
and dance daringly and drearily with worthy restraints
but she soberly scorned my sagely suggestions
and hiked hurriedly towards the tarred traps
that got her harvesting tears like tailored taps.

Life is a trap
sordidly spread with gaps.
It feels like rosy road
to some and like toads
carefreely hitting herself on the ground

as she through life's chambered fount.
The first wife dances with care
and her co-wives pout as she dances and dare.
My sister if you must dance
my brother, if you have got chance
to be bountifully blessed beyond brim
with life's fount that dispel grin
Do not, I pray you, lonely lavish
do not, I entreat you, greedily gulp or ravish
the towering life's largesse
like the Chinese mayonnaise.
Call your neighbours to join you
in licking the finger full of honey.
Call your kindreds to harvest the basket full of money.
Life is a magnificent mirror
that magnificently magnify mundane errors
like a somnolent spy ready to unleash terror.
If you see your stiffed self and face through it
let others see what you singularly saw.
Let them explore and extol your store.
If you wear the world like a pant
do not, kindreds, travel or pant
with world's withering grant
lonely on the meandering meadow without a chant.

SEMAPHORE OF THE FLOUNDERING SHIP

Fling open the iron-gate
of the central power cage
at all cost and raging rate
that southpoles and northpoles
may be belligerently beguiled and cajoled
of the unequal equity that characterised
the race to pacify the pauperised
and over-fed delicate delegates
Who caroused at food-store of the power-cage.
That was the charge from the pompous pope
of the hallowed house of Kojole
a name synonymous with plundering
a personality akin to fathomless floundering.
The gate was flagrantly flung open
for all delegated devils of the Umbrelland
to attend and hike with the dollar-doned drones.
The feast was presided upon by poverty-prone
officiants on thorn-doned crowns thrones.
Now, the serpent that was sent out of Eden
has smuggled himself and his offspring
into the ship stirring sinister scatterings.
This sinister scheming snowballed into ship-
sinking.

Now they've sold their collective conscience
like those who think equity is a rocket science
and all the juicy cakes hauled to the Upper
Niger,
southern scoundrels and oafish officiants rant
of staying in the ship and sink her with her
flanks.

TO THE KETTLE CALLING POT BLACK

Do not see me as a sinner
feasting on sins like dinner.
We are all carefree culprits
mounting ubiquitous pulpits.
If you are not randy
and you are a lover of brandy,
we all transgress
We all digress
scorning scrupulous audits
in covetous craze for plaudits.

You do not romance mischief
But you are a twin sister of unbelief.
You do not lie,
Yet you buy bribes
In form of tithes
sucking like lordless lice.
You do not steal
yet, from swindlers you swindle stolen seed.
You do not collect percentages
but your altars feast fat on sinful syndicates.

You indulge not in bloodshed
but collect proceeds from every head

in form of offerings and first fruits
and righteousness you scorn like brutes.
You are the twin brother of Chichidodo.
You abhor farts and fattening faeces
yet, on its maggots you feast
like cruel communicants coveting Eucharistic elements.
You sell lies like limestone to people of governments
to petrify the pockets of your covetuous cassocks
as you ply the hell-bent pilgrimages.
You scorn pure piety
and bethrot your souls to gory gaiety.

All our piety and riotous righteousness
are nothing but stinking and tattered togas.
You are not an armed robber
yet you finagle widow's mite without rudder
and justify the daylight defrauding
with verses from holy books
flowing from you like the brooks.
One who defends devil is a devil himself.
You are not a terrorist or bandit
but you are the bandit's advocate.

We are all sinking sinners
with our guilts gorgeously swinging
like the albatross in the Mariners' mime.
If our propitiations to the arch-deity
is rejected, condemned we are without mercy.

Okitipupa, turning ASUU strike into blessings,August 14, 2022.

IF I SUSPECT YOU

I will not break my vow
In order to offer a bow
I will not lie lifelessly low
just to eat the meat of a cow
I will not betray my circumspection
To feign humility in the name of genuflection.
Ile aye ti le: life is as complicated as a crisscross
full of suspicion and animosity so gross
that no one can now be trusted.
Kindreds, I beseech you, if I suspect you
if I circumvent my initial respect for you
in the manner of a lily-livered ewe
who always fears that she will be slain
on the merciless slaughter-slab in vain
be not confounded
let not your peace be compounded.
That's the vogue security consciousness
begotten by the contemporary craze of get-rich-at-all-cost
in every gamut of trust for anyone is shattered and lost,
in which brother betray brother and sell each other like loaves.

Okitipupa, turning ASUU strike into blessings, August 16, 2022.

REIGN OF THE IDIOTS AND RASCALS

The wise claim to be too tutored
The sage claim to be too cultured
the elite claim to be too schooled
the rich rant to be too tooled
The teachers think that they are too tailored
and leave the rule of the land to the fools.
The vine dressers are too puffed up
with the gaiety of their wine shop
and indiscriminately jettison their voluptuous
vineyards
to novices in the discernment of good and bad
wine.

Those thoroughly tutored teenage descendants
of the famous farmers forsake farming and
abandon the selection of tubers good enough
for pounded yam to inconsiderable ignoramuses
who, instead of bringing fine tubers for the
dinner,
bring warty watery yam tubers, only to instigate
rancor.
The skillful fishermen forsake fishing, leaving
the

the science and art of fishing to foolish
fishermen
who are bereft of ideas of fishing and cannot
tell eels from feigning and sprawling snakes.
Those of noble birth become nobler than
nobility
and cede to the silly slaves their royal utility
only to wake to the dawn of reign of the idiots
who rule royalty like rutherless ruins and
maggots.
Kindreds, if you are too holy or you feel that
your
royal robes are too pure for the noble cause

of leading your kiths with sagely sanity through
the stalls of the of the palm oil merchants
into eldorado, the idiots will not only usurp
throne bequeathed to you by benevolent
progenitors
but will also soil your garments and dignity
and eventually turn upside down your royal
ancestry.
Rule your world or you'll be ruled out of order.

IF THE PEOPLE STAND

My dear people perish
with no one to cherish.
They bend bastard-like, bamboozled
under the poli-tricksters' table,
led like loyal lambs to the sinful stable.
The people know not the power
in their tireless thumbs and hover
around like waywardly whirled wings.
With silly songs they dance in ring
as they ignorantly hunch under the table
the poli-tricksters preponderantly feast
on the collectively coveted cakes
and wash down the bountiful bites
with voluptuous vinegars and
intermittently sandwich it with wastefully
purchased ponche and fattened ox-meat.
As they flamboyantly feast with dubious debauchery
they feed the people on whose shoulders they ride
to stardom with waning and crunchy crumbs.
The day the people know the power of their thumbs
they will only have to stand on their feet
and turn the table against the tricksters.
Guess what!
It is feast over and game-halt.

ANOTHER HOLOCAUST LOOMING

For ASUU and all victims of incessant ASUU strikes in Nigeria where the political class deliberately depopulate public institutions in order to populate their ill-fated mushroom private universities, midwived out of wickedness of keeping the children of the masses perpetually out of schools.

I see another holocaust haughtily looming
I see another bombastic bomb booming.
The war will not be between the Nazis
and the hated hermits, servile Semites,
murderous moors or the jejune Jews
The war will be fought by the children
of the uneducated and uncultured kindreds
whose education the arrant aristocrats
who think they have crossed the rubicon
ruthlessly refused to invest upon.
The war may not end till the last
child of the oligarchs and aristocrats
standing had been clubbed or mowed
down by the livid legion of the ill-educated
children of the poor or streets urchins.
If the rich or the royalty think they are safe
by wrecking the education of the slaves,

they have only bought and kept cute coffins
for their own over-pampered and well-nurtured
kids.
If only Nigerian cruel cooks
no that they are banally breeding crooks
by being indiscriminate towards home
books they will let the children of poor

live that theirs may live in peace.
They will not be building drifting domes
for their children and treat the poors like gnomes.
They will know that those who wish to eat good
broth
behind secured doors do not need those doors.
All they need is to prepare enough for all to bloat.
Iron doors will be brazenly barren and impotent
for the safety of the oppressors like the seashore
sand
in the cruel and whirling hands of the heedless
wind
by the time the wasting wrath the oppressed
sprouts and
ripens rapaciously, devoid of restive redress.

JUST WITHOUT LULL

Just without lasting lull
will the world be.
Just without musing mull
will the sea be
without pontificating poetry
and without mystical moiety
that snowballs somnolently into gaiety.
The world will wallow without worth
and without wondrously welling words
wrapped in the gorgeous garb of brevity
and compressed into verses and bites
of lulling lollipops licked lewedly like
the baby's suck of the mother's breasts.
Poetry is the sea of lovable lullabies
into which the world is wrapped like cannabis
that sweetens the throats of the smokers.
Prose peers and pierces into the erring ears
of the ceaselessly erring listeners and readers
as It ministers only to their ears and meanders
away like the musketeering moonlight and
twilight.
Drama walks and talks before buoyant eyes
of the audience and viewers like thawing ice.
It flippantly frets from and to the stage

of human scorning sight like misty mirage.
Poetry gores gracefully into the garage
of the human soul and the eternal essence
of his psychical foetus like the fuming fragrance
of the roomy chamber and of the rapacious roses
taken like libidinous librum in dotting doses.
Poetry is born, a son and sun of necessity
so that the world may never go to slumber
or be bewildered belligerently like obesity,
on empty stomach like loafing lumber,
devoid of impetuous inspiration or infatuation.
Poetry is world's lullaby and consolation
in all turbulent tantrums and sorry situations.

Akungba-Akoko, turning ASUU strike into blessings, August 23, 2022.

ON YOUR TRACK!

Return, I insist, to your track.
Get onto your meandering mark
and get set for yet another race
that can only be accomplished by greater grace.

Run again, brethren, with zealous zest
even as you crave not your restive rest,
strive strenuously for luminous loft
and race with ovulating strength, even though
you are soft.

Reckon not with the day's doleful gloom.
The world awaits your pregnant plaudits and
bloom
and to ceaselessly celebrate your garlands and
laurels
won by sedulously scorning the beauteous
barrels.

Remember that the world acknowledges only
hailing
they care not about your losses and flatulent
failings.

Will you rise and strive scrupulously towards a goal?
Move now and dismantle riling roadblocks as you go!

THIS TIME SHALL PASS

Surely shall this sultry sun set
and deadened drearily into a bet
for furious future and fortunate fruition.
Surely shall this tortuous tempest trotter
into oblivion, for the birth of an infant dawn.

This time of working without wages wrought
by the white-bearded baron and the members
of his first and callous caliphate who wish to live
that others may be impoverished or cease to live.
Truly, today tortures our tomorrows to the
fallopian
tube of the terror-stricken tents, yet we await a
utopia.

This time that works wondrous wonders for the
bad
and not for the beautiful ones borne by
circumstances,
this time that works for the sworn enemies of the
state
against the obedient, who work in all earnestness
to brace

the state from being submerged into the vagina of ruin
shall re-emerge like the fortunate phoenix from the ashes.

I entreat you, therefore, compatriots, arise,
gird yourselves with loins of faith and rise aright
in the assauging assurance that a virgin dawn
shall be borne out of the ashes of the burnt lawn.
Laugh, kindreds, laugh, in anticipation of the dawn
that will roost like the apparitions of the sheep
from the ruins at the slaughter-slab.

We'll wear rosy ribbon through this dusk that's drab.

This time, this tardy tide, my battered brethren,
shall surely sweep surreptitiously, souless sentinels
that foisted this time tyrannical tide on us away and AWOL.
This time shall surely pass, brethren, and our gory
sores shall be drowned by undying and glamorous glory.

THE STAINLESS SLAUGHTER SLAB

When harmattan fires burns tortured tinders
in the forest, the fire flakes are the tell-tales
hither.
A female is never christened Kumolu without a
mystery
A woman who gives birth to a "*nonulet*"
has impregnated history
just the way a dancer who jumps
\up has beheaded and buried dance.

I heard that the descendants of *Akegbajalu*
visited *Kuje*
in fury but left there, gallivanting to the rocuous
rhythm
of the talking drums that never sounded from
the birth
and death of the bloodless war stage-managed
by
the kinsmen of the Primate to free the wards of
A-soro-i-pa.

To be frank, they came, sure, with riffles and
AK-47 to

the ceremonious cantata of freeing the remanded
reverends
of *Kuje* temple and the walls of the temple
opened their mouths
and emptied their bountiful bowels and
intestines with cloudy clouts.

No gutting gunshot to threaten the
sentinels of the truth tending
the temple or the thieving
state-sent sentries from the birth to the
death of the cantata of freedom
and exodus from Egypt and Babylon.
Only songs of freedom rent the air
with admixture of bullying belief and
Thomas-like disbelief caressed
the ears and minds of impetuous and
inquisitive folks of the film-trick nation
wherein terrorists traversed and
trampled upon the impregnable
prison walls without pulling a trigger.
No be juju or film trick be that?
If you ask me, that is one of the
seven wonders of the 21st century
Naija and such film tricks can only
find a putrid patronage here and here alone,

that cowed cows were silently slaughtered
without blood-stains on unblemished slaughter-
slab.

FOOTNOTE:

A-soro-i-pa means one who is difficult to kill.
Akegbajalu means the bandits and terrorists

VIRTUE AND VICES DON'T DIE

Virtue and vices don't die
They only go on sabbatical for a while
They return to stare us in the face
even as they hasten their pace
from the land of oblivion, not to hide
any more because they are rile.
Truth and falsehood rear their heads
again when they are ripe enough for harvest.

They sprout like seeds sown on the Everest.
The pains and gains they give are like oil
For they never hide or flinch on the marble.
Tell, therefore, those who defecate at the
market,
Tell again, those who shamelessly urinate on the
altar
to anticipate a recompence for them and their
seeds
for every deed is a seed sown in pregnant hope
of a seed.

I'M OGBUULU: A POETIC HISTORIOGRAPHY

Oramfe, lord of the house of fire
grew stout-hearted and towered higher
above waters and *Ora* hills.
He soared above the frills.
He mated with mountains
and impregnated the fountains.

The unions begot warriors
The coitus ripened into midwifery of
conquistadors
and the connubial conjugation conjured farmers.
The polygamy preponderantly produced
poachers
and fishermen who later married the rivers
and fathered fervent folks by *Okun-liri.*

They roosted and continue to roost
on the chest of the Atlantic Ocean
as if in an eternal coital romps and spree
The rivers and waters they have for a boost.
There, in-between the languid limbs of the sea
and the bounteous breasts of the creeks

they burgeoned exceedingly unhinged
like the waves of the sedulous sea
and the fluidity of the gorgeously flowing fluid
that make perfect paths among the wondrous
woods.
Frolicsome folks around them admire
their mirthful miens with insatiable desire
as they covetously covet their girth,
heroic peregrinations and noble birth.

Through the crested creeks
they traversed like the troubadours of the
Greeks.
Through the thick and thin mangrove forests
they thrusted their tender tentacles
to deflower every physical and metaphysical
obstacle
and they had *Mafunrangan* for a cradle,
like the Everest.

On the limbs of the Atlantic Ocean,
they flourish fervidly, like the fiery furnace
devouring the hymen and forest's appurtenances
without being merciful or mean.

Their neighbours noisomely name them
Ogbuulu
a titular appellation and cognomen synonymous
with mystiques, geniality and imperturbable
run of waters and damnable deluge.
We are proud of whom the world calls us
and who we really are, like cactus spectabilis.

Ubiquitously unruffled, we veil two hundred
poles
at war, festive and peacetimes for fortification
of our souls
to humongously herald our affluence and
heritage
too invincible for human plundering and
sabotage.
Ogbuulu! *Ogbuulu!! Ogbuulu*!!!
Ogbuulu mi je!

www.ingramcontent.com/pod-product-compliance
Lightning Source LLC
LaVergne TN
LVHW091110150826
845673LV00002B/764

9789787940532